# Seven
# Sayings
# of Jesus

---

## HOW ONE MAN'S WORDS
## CAN CHANGE YOUR WORLD

By Harry T. Cook

**VANTAGE PRESS**
New York

Other titles by Harry T. Cook:

*Christianity Beyond Creeds* (1997): ISBN 0-9660728-0-4
*Sermons of a Devoted Heretic* (1999): ISBN 0-9660728-1-2

The above titles and more information are available through:

Center for Rational Christianity
P.O. Box 182
Clawson, MI 48017

FIRST EDITION

Published by Vantage Press, Inc.
516 West 34th Street, New York, New York 10001

Manufactured in the United States of America
ISBN: 0-533-13979-1

Library of Congress Catalog Card No.: 01-130621

0 9 8 7 6 5 4 3 2 1

*For*
*Dainforth Baker French*
*and*
*Paul B. Hessert*

*In memoriam*

# Table of Contents

# Preface

I first became acquainted with the inquiry, "What would Jesus do?" when my younger children came home from church camp one summer with bracelets bearing the legend "WWJD." I learned from my kids that those initials and the words they represent had been the programmatic theme of the camp week.

Not ordinarily fond of gimmicks, my initial reaction was mild, amused tolerance. Upon reflection, though, I began to appreciate the value of such a deceptively simple pedagogical approach. What is key, however, is an unblinkered appreciation of who Jesus was and wasn't, what he may or may not have said and how to get at all that in an intellectually responsible way.

What better question for a follower of Jesus to pose when faced with important choices and decisions? If the teaching of Jesus is received as some expression of how the world is meant to work, then what Jesus would do – if such a thing can be discerned – is of utmost importance. Thus, this book.

A first chapter explores the question "Who was Jesus?" Relying on the contributions of several contemporary Jesus scholars, *e.g.*, John Dominic Crossan, E.P. Sanders, John Meier, Elisabeth Schussler Fiorenza and Marcus Borg – as those have, in this author's view, tried to give wide berth to theological agenda in favor of evidence – I try to give an accessible picture of Jesus.

With that as foundation, a second chapter looks at seven primary sayings that may reasonably be attributed to Jesus. With an as clear as possible sense of what Jesus may have said established, one may better determine what he would, in fact, do.

A third chapter is a defense of the importance of Jesus today, of why Jesus matters now.

A fourth chapter will unfold a series of vignettes culled from years of experience and observation – instances in which persons struggled with critical choices and decisions. The conclusions which they reached or to which they were guided are each and all situational, *i.e.*, not binding on others in different situations but the "right" conclusion for the concluder at the time.

It is the underlying assumption of this book that most moral choices are made in that manner, *viz.*, by consulting the fundamental prescriptive values in which one believes and by which one tries to live, by looking at the situation at hand to see who will be helped or hurt by the contemplated choice and finally by adjusting the terms of the choice so as to control its consequences with the greatest good for the greatest number of paramount concern.

The fifth and final chapter will note parallels in secular thought of what will be called the ethic of the seven Jesus sayings.

A word about the length of this and my other books. Each of them was at least twice the length of what turned out to be the finished product, but kindly advice from people whose wisdom I trust has in each case caused me to rely on my several years' experience as a newspaper writer and columnist. That experience taught me to write concisely for the attention span of late 20th Century readers. With almost every paragraph I have had to resist the impulse to add or expand material, preferring to state matters as concisely as possible while being as complete as possible. The goal, my counselors say, is to get people to read the book, not be intimidated by it.

As with everything I attempt to commit to publication, I am forever indebted to my wife of 21 years, Sue Chevalier, who is also my editor and the designer of my books. Uncredited in the last two but without whose diligence neither of the previous two books nor this book could have been published is my co-worker, Lois Skora, who has successfully decoded my fountain-pen script with the skill of a cryptologist and typed the manuscripts.

"What would Jesus do?" is a valid, yea, critical question for those who find themselves somewhere in the Christian ethical sphere. The question is really a Jewish one because so much of who Jesus was is derivative of the Hebrew prophets and others in that tradition. Perhaps the most quoted of the sayings reasonably attributed to Jesus is some variation on, "Do unto others as you would have done to yourself." The venerable Hillel's "What you would not have done to you do not do to another" was clearly an inspiration for Jesus.

So what the question "What would Jesus do?" really asks is what would a god of the Hebrew-Christian scriptures will. That is why the question goes beyond a church camp gimmick.

— *Harry T. Cook*

Chapter One
# Who Was Jesus?

The historic creeds of the church and a good bit of its preaching and teaching over the centuries answer the question of Jesus' identity by proclaiming that he was (and is) the Son of God – the one-time, exclusive disclosure of the One God's will and purpose. The fourth evangelist known as John went so far as to say that Jesus was, in fact, the eternal logos, *i.e.*, the organizing and creative principle of the universe in human form: "And the logos became flesh and dwelt among us" (John 1:14).

John then goes on to tell his version of Jesus' story which in some respects follows the general plot line originally proposed by Mark. Little in John's story line seems to support the startling proclamation of 1:14. In both John and the synoptic gospels the terms "Son of man" and "Son of God" are interplayed with much suggested by indirection.

The picture Mark paints of Jesus is of a religious counter-cultural presence upsetting the scribal apple cart by his appearance in the Capernaum synagogue (Mark 2:1-12). It is Mark who first reports (or concocts) Jesus saying: "It is easier for a camel to squeeze through a needle's eye than for a rich one to be admitted to God's dominion" (Mark 10:25, parallels Matthew 19:24, Luke 18:25).

Matthew seemed more interested in connecting Jesus to the pre-First Century C.E. Jewish past and identifying him with Abraham (1:1) and David (*ibid*) and as the saving messiah (2:20b-22). Luke picks up on some of that but seems to expand its scope beyond the concerns of Israel. For Luke, Jesus is not only the scion of Abraham and David but of primal humankind (3:38b). We have already seen what John's take on Jesus was.

Paul rather quickly brought a figure he often calls "Christ Jesus" into a mythic formula familiar to most First Century C.E. religions, *viz.*, as the dying and rising Son of God (Romans 5:6-11, 6:9-10, I Corinthians 15:20-28, Colossians 1:15-23).

The church incorporated these various images into a

theological system expressed in the historic creeds and asks of its members belief in those terms. I was part of a clergy conversation recently in which "the divinity of Christ" was the topic. The author whose book was under discussion was, despite his monumental erudition, virtually dismissed because his research and analysis led him away from any such a priori claim that Jesus had been something other than human. Is it any wonder that it is difficult to answer the question "What would Jesus do?" when there is little agreement about who he was, what he said and what it means?

I put the question "Who was Jesus?" to a rabbi friend of mine. His answer was, "One of us." That obvious fact seems perennially to get lost in the shuffle. Whatever else Jesus may have been or have been proclaimed to be, he was a Jew, though not a Judean, probably of what John Dominic Crossan terms the "landless laborer" class (**The Birth of Christianity**, p. 350). Most textual evidence suggests that he was a Nazarene Galilean born somewhere around the millenium shift (6 B.C.E. - 4 C.E.). His emergence in the Galilee toward the end of the first third of the First Century C.E. was either coincidental with or connected to the massive economic dislocations of that era as two Roman cities (Sepphoris and Tiberias) were under massive construction in an otherwise agrarian region.

Crossan understands the emergence of Jesus as a part of the peasant resistance to forced urbanization during the reign of Herod Antipas (*op.cit,* p. 231). Even N.T. Wright agrees in part: "(Jesus) was not so much like a wandering preacher giving sermons or a wandering philosopher offering maxims as like a radical politician gathering support for a new and highly risky movement " (**The Meaning of Jesus**, Marcus J. Borg and N.T. Wright, p.36). Wright goes on to connect Jesus' political analysis with a theological program featuring Yahweh as king as opposed to Caesar or his minions.

E.P.Sanders, usually appreciated as a conservative scholar, more or less accepts as historical much of the gospel narrative, though not the nativity narratives of Matthew and Luke. Sanders does not attempt, indeed resists an attempt, to paint a whole picture of Jesus. Anything on that order, he says, would be a "partial at best" (**The Historical Figure of Jesus**, p. 76). Sanders uses the phrase "indisputable facts" to describe the following reports in the gospels: Jesus lived with his parents in Nazareth of Galilee, was baptized by John, began his own public ministry at about the time John was executed, preached in villages, healed the sick, rode into Jerusalem on an ass, had his temper tantrum in the Temple, had Passover with his friends, was arrested, tried, turned over to the Romans and was crucified. Subsequently his disciples had "resurrection experiences" — whatever they might have been — which persuaded them that, whatever happened to Jesus, he would come back to complete his salvific work.

John Meier is a priest of the Roman Catholic Church. His **A Marginal Jew** attempts, he says, to entertain the singular question, "Who did Jesus think he was?" Meier's answer is that Jesus was pushed to the margins of society by the Jewish (religious) and Roman (political) power structures because of his proclamation that the rule of God — as opposed to the rule of Torah as construed by scribes and Pharisees and the rule of Caesar — is both a future and a present reality. This latter is shown forth in Jesus' miracles. Meier is strong on the so-called miracles as having actually occurred.

Elisabeth Schussler Fiorenza of the Harvard Divinity School is best known by her 1984 **Bread, Not Stone: ... In Memory of Her** and the 1994 **Jesus: Miriam's Child, Sophia's Prophet**. Beyond Fiorenza's strong feminist advocacy and her distrust of many New Testament texts as androcentrically and patriarchally biased is her view of Jesus

17

as one who taught that the rule of God was present and available as experiential reality. For Fiorenza, Jesus was a prophetic and radical egalitarian opposed to male domination and inevitably patriarchal hierarchies. Jesus was the designated prophet of Sophia – wisdom – and, as such, a feminine reality in a masculine persona. Out of such wisdom, Jesus advocated equality of the sexes and classes. (**Bread, Not Stone**, p. 148)

Crossan, emeritus professor of religious studies at Chicago's DePaul University, is among the most eminent New Testament scholars of this era – certainly where Jesus studies are concerned. His is a thoroughly historical approach often described as interdiscipliary in nature. Out of that immersion, Crossan developed the hypothesis that Jesus was an itinerant street speaker, a counter-cultural fly-in-the ointment type. For Crossan, Jesus was of peasant stock, perhaps, as we have seen above, landless and therefore on the margins between poverty and destitution. Jesus was a subversive in Crossan's view who made a point of sharing meals with people regardless of social class and custom. Out of such experiences, Crossan says, came the Christian eucharist – or, as he says, "the share meal" – but what the gospels report as the

Last Supper is purely fictional. So, too, the resurrection. Crossan's research and analysis suggest to him that Jesus' execution was the final word, that his body was not buried but left, as the final insult, to be eaten by wild dogs.

Marcus J. Borg teaches religion and culture at Oregon State University. He is a member of the Jesus Seminar and has chaired the Society of Biblical Literature's Historical Jesus committee. For Borg, the historical Jesus was a Jew through and through. Borg says we "know" Jesus was born around the beginning of the millennium (plus or minus 4 B.C.E.), that he was reared in the lower Galilee and had parents named Joseph and Mary. How we "know" that Borg doesn't say. He thinks Jesus did not see himself as a messianic figure. Borg's Jesus was moved by an existential awareness of God's presence out of which proceeded wisdom teachings regarding human behavior and a prophetic message concerning social and economic dislocation. Borg does not think Jesus' message was given for the purpose of leading people to heaven or that Jesus was in any way resurrected. Borg's important works include **Jesus, A New Vision** (1987), **Jesus In Contemporary Scholarship** (1994), and **Meeting Jesus Again for the First Time** (1994).

So who was Jesus? The answer to that question will be different from that to the question of, "Who has Jesus become?" Jesus has become pretty much what various people, interest groups and denominations have wanted him to become. To the composers of 19th Century Protestant hymns he was a "precious savior still our refuge," "the dear Lord I adore," one calling "softly and tenderly" to the abject sinner, and so on and so on. To the proponents of 20th Century liberation theology, Jesus has become the model for Caesar Chavez. To liberals such as I, Jesus has become the spirit of a humanistic ethic whose foundation is the Golden Rule. All well and good, but who was Jesus?

Almost definitely not the person variously depicted by the writers of the canonical gospels. While Mark, Matthew and Luke seem to depict the same person, they depict him differently owing, one supposes, to the necessities of their own time and place. The Jesus depicted in the Fourth Gospel is in many respects the antithesis of the synoptic Jesus. The Gospel of Thomas represents a kind of rough-hewn, provocative and cryptic, almost phantom Jesus. Josephus devotes a mere 125 words to him (**Antiquities of the Jews,** 18.3.3), and Suetonius wrote of one "Chrestus" and Tacitus of "Christus."

What, then, is the most educated guess as to who Jesus was? Perhaps this: Jesus was of Galilean peasant stock, a self-taught person with a well-formed social conscience in the tradition of the first Isaiah, Amos and Micah. He chose the mien of the itinerant cynic as the medium of his message, *viz.*, he traveled from settlement to settlement after the fashion spelled out in Mark 6:8: "No bread, no bag, no money in belts, no extra tunic." This was to make him accessible and vulnerable to the communities he visited, not self-sufficient but bearing only the power of his message. That message could best be summed up in seven sayings that, taken together, represent a coherent, humanistic ethic: Turn the other cheek, walk the second mile, give up your shirt as well as your coat, forgive seventy times seven, love your neighbor, love your enemy and do to others what you would have done to you.

How that ethic played in the Galilee in the first third of the First Century C.E. depended on who was hearing it expounded. To those on the line between mere poverty and abject destitution it must have been as much of a mystery as to those who were not. We will examine those sayings individually and at greater length in the next chapter, but suffice it for now to observe that the ethic outlined in those sayings is almost other-worldly in that the world we know just doesn't ordinarily work that way. A blow to the cheek is highly likely to produce a counter punch, and, as for walking the second mile, it is not within commonplace human disposition to walk the first if it can possibly be avoided.

Jesus, apparently, was a person who believed that human nature was not necessarily what it seemed to be but was capable of far more and at a higher level of responsibility and enlightenment than ordinarily thought. Those seven sayings suggest that it is possible for human beings to behave in the manner indicated by them. Jesus would then have been an ethical visionary who, long before the Renaissance of the Second Millennium, came to see that, far from being hopelessly depraved, humankind had the natural potential to live in collective respect and charity in an Eden-like setting, that redemption, like "the kingdom of God," is within the human being waiting to come out or to be let out.

The canonical gospels – all of them – depict Jesus as having been the victim of public hostility and, eventually, of a scornful Judean establishment and a ruthless Roman military government. He is depicted as a blasphemer, iconoclast and seditionist. If the gospels are any indication of the historical Jesus' public exposure, it was almost entirely what he is said to have expressed verbally that brought him into confrontation with the powers that were. We can then understand that his moral ethos was seen as subversive and threatening. How the actual Jesus, whoever and whatever he might have been, was dealt with, what the actual cause of his demise, it is clear that his impact was felt well beyond the time of his death, and that successive generations, beginning with his supposed sayings circulated early on in the hypothetical document known as "Q" (Ger., quelle or source) which is embedded in Matthew and Luke, as well as in a similar collection known as the Gospel of Thomas, have built an entire religion on his continuously re-created person.

We do not, in the end, have much of an idea of who Jesus was and even less about his life. We can assume he was a Galilean Jew who came to public attention toward the end of the first third of the First Century – a time of economic and political tumult in the region, to which his public utterances and activities may have been responses. Beyond that, anything we say is at best creative fiction and, at worst, deliberate concoction.

Chapter Two
# What Did Jesus Say?

We have already seen the monumental difficulties in determining with any certainty anything the one called Jesus might have said. With the Jesus Seminar, we might better look for some consistency among all the so-called "red letter" sayings around which over time textual editors have placed quotation marks, so attributing them to Jesus.

We have suggested that he was an exponent of a peculiar humanistic ethic, that such was his possible distinction among many of his itinerant street-speaker types. Working from that hypothesis, it is possible to find that consistency in seven sayings that may be actual utterances or derivative of stories attributed by tradition to Jesus.

Those sayings are:

- Turn the other cheek (Matthew 5:39, Luke 6:29);
- Walk the second mile (Matthew 5:41);
- Give up your shirt as well as your coat (Matthew 5:40, Luke 6:29);
- Forgive 70 times seven (Matthew 18:22, Luke 17:4);
- Love your neighbor (Mark 12:31, 33, Matthew 5:43, 19:19, 22:39, Luke 10:27ff)
- Love your enemy (Matthew 5:44, Luke 6:27);
- Do to others as you would have done to yourself (Matthew 7:12, Luke 6:31).

In what actual, original context Jesus may have uttered such sayings, or out of what reality any of them may have been appropriately attributed to him cannot be known. But the seven sayings above are ethically consistent and envision a kind of society that could aptly be called "the kingdom of God" or "people living under the rule of God" – "God" being that largely benign presence to which Israel began to bear witness in its communal life earlier on in its existence. The central thesis of this book is that these seven sayings say as much about the actual Jesus as he was remembered by his earliest followers as anything we possess in the scriptural tradition. Who Jesus was

– and therefore what he would do – can reasonably be distilled from an understanding and appreciation of these sayings.

## Turn the other cheek

In the Mediterranean culture, the striking of a person's right cheek with the back of the hand is a well-known and established major insult. According to Joachim Jeremias (**The Sermon on the Mount**) the action was administered to one thought to be a heretic. Even today, the gesture is explosively provocative. Not only does it inflict sharp pain, it can break the skin, damage teeth and even cause neurological trauma. Basic human instinct is to strike back defensively or to protect oneself from further blows. By turning the other (or left) cheek, the victim passively asserts himself and his dignity by presenting his face for another attack, daring the attacker to strike again.

The late Martin Luther King, Jr. was once struck across the face by an angry sheriff's officer. Those who watched braced themselves for some response, if not from King, then from his supporters who were present. In that electric moment, as in the nanosecond of silence between the bolt of lightning and the resultant thunderclap, almost anything might have happened. What did happen was that King shook himself slightly as if to regain composure and thus ever so slightly turned his head, presenting the other side of his face to the sheriff's officer. That was too much for the officer. He had nothing to do but to stare inchoately into King's eyes, shrug dumbly and shamble away. Whose dignity shone forth that day? By what act was serious violence prevented? Who was in charge?

To my knowledge, King never explained his action (or inaction) on that occasion. Perhaps no one dared ask him about it. But as a minister of the gospel, he clearly seemed to have been practicing the passive resistance he claimed to find in the teachings and example of Jesus of Nazareth. Not that turning the other cheek always works out the way it did with King that day. As often as not, the other cheek gets it twice as hard as the first – perhaps because the turning of the other cheek so provokes the attacker that he strikes back in double anger. Perhaps he perceives in the cheek-turning a defiance of his might. Of course, that's what the turned cheek is: defiance and the tacit determination that might will not make right no matter how much force is applied. It is the statement that violence will not be met with violence, or blow for blow. Turned enough times, the smitten cheek becomes a powerful rebuke of the attacker and eventually shames him into the cessation of hostilities. Massive passive resistance eventually gets the attention of even the most determined aggressor. Shame eventually overtakes him and, if he does not back off, the world forces him to back off, because decency is finally a human mandate.

Tragically, persistent passive resistance can issue in serious injury and terrible loss of life before shame and the mandate for decency assert themselves.

Turning the other cheek is a very difficult aspect of the Jesus ethic and is generally not the norm. But enough people turning enough cheeks will eventually become a majority. To put it in the patois of contemporary adolescents, when enough people are put under peer pressure to do a thing, it become "cool." It seizes the day and wins it. The "thing" is not spoken of so much as it is acted out. In the acting out of it, it becomes a working example, and, as it catches on, it becomes the norm. When turning the other cheek becomes the norm in any community small or great, it could reasonably be said, in New Testament language, that the kingdom of God has truly dawned.

## Walk the second mile

In First Century C.E. Palestine the power with which to reckon at all levels was the Roman political military establishment. Its baleful influence was everywhere felt. The construction over two decades of two major Roman cities (Sepphoris and Tiberius) only 20 miles apart apparently caused great economic dislocation with land and crop confiscation and conscripted labor. The military's word however and by whom it was spoken was law. That is the probable social context for the saying about walking the second mile. It was evidently part of martial law that a Roman soldier could commandeer a non-Roman citizen to carry his gear for the equivalent of one of our 5,280-foot miles. Never mind what burden the conscript was already bearing and under what circumstances. The gear of a centurion could not have been anything but heavy and cumbersome.

Even a peasant accustomed to rude and overbearing treatment would surely have found the order to bear the soldier's gear deeply offensive and oppressive. That, briefly, is the immediate context of this Jesus saying.

Why might he have counseled the voluntary second mile? Two possibilities come to mind: a) to spare another the task and b) to serve as an act of passive resistance – not to the order itself but to the idea that the soldier held any enduring power over the conscript. One can envision a child of tender years or an aged person being drafted to carry the soldier's gear. If a more able-bodied person had gotten through the first mile, perhaps the volunteering of the second mile to spare the youth or elder the grueling task would have been indicated. But I am more attracted to the second possibility because it is reminiscent of the turned cheek.

Perhaps Jesus was saying that the volunteered second mile would be so arresting an offer that it could begin the process of turning an enemy into a friend, or at least a non-enemy. The offer to go the second mile might be so disarming to a Roman soldier who, after all, would have been only another human being perhaps far from home, that he might want to know more about this strange Galilean or Judean. It is a one-on-one kind of conversion that is envisioned here, but I don't know how else conversion really works except one at a time. Certainly the first person who may have volunteered the second mile would have been considered to be a masochist or otherwise deranged. It's always difficult to be the one who challenges the norm first, who does the utterly unexpected thing. It can be costly and it often doesn't have what may be the desired effect at first. So the one who contemplates the second-mile offer needs to know from the start that the offer might be spurned, that it might be considered subversive and that it might invite more trouble than it would appear to be worth.

Yet another possibility is that a community of the like-minded may covenant all to make the offer and actually begin to undertake the walk, with or without the burden. Such gestures have been known to move the unmovable. And while real conversion comes one person at a time, a company of converted ones is able to make a statement that is hard to ignore. Gandhi's march to the sea to make salt set the Raj on its ear and rendered it well-nigh helpless even though it possessed the military and political power. Similarly a committed majority offering to go the second mile could render such a mandate meaningless and assert the dignity of those who make the offer. It is one way that the mighty can be put down from their seats, the humble and meek exalted, the valleys raised up and the mountains and hills made low. Some would say such equity would amount to the glory of the Lord which all flesh might witness together.

## Give up your shirt as well as your coat

The context here is economic. Crossan suggests that the saying might originally have been heard, "Give up your one shirt as well as your one coat." It is difficult for almost any American to appreciate the reality of that. Even where the so-called poverty line for a family of four is $17,000 per annum or thereabouts, the idea of having but one inner garment and one outer garment would seem strange. In a world of rummage sales, Salvation Army stores and used clothing emporia amply supplied by an affluent middle class of the throw-away generation, one shirt and one shirt only may not compute. But among peasant Palestinians of the First Century C.E., such straitened circumstances were evidently common. Crossan talks of "the thin line" that separated the merely poor from the destitute. The poor would have one shirt and one coat. The destitute might have neither. That's what makes contemporary sense of the Matthean passage, "When I was naked, you clothed me ..." In the First Century, it was quite possible to have no clothing. And when one considers that Hebraic abhorrence of nakedness, giving up one's only shirt as well as one's only coat takes on significance beyond economics.

What is the net gain in giving up one's entire wardrobe upon request? One formerly unclad body becomes clothed, and one formerly clad becomes naked. Is the saying a deliberate overstatement? And, if so, what was the intent? It could not have been an economic plan to redistribute the sartorial wealth(?) of the peasant populace. There was an obvious shortage. If one had shirt and coat, and another had neither, why not give up either shirt or coat, so two people would have some sort of raiment? That would be what we in America idiomatically term "going 50-50," which seems a fairly intelligent way to deal with a shortage. Yet the mandate is to give up shirt and coat. Jesus' way seemed never to have been 50-50 but 100-100. Having was desirable only so one could give. Giving was life. Keeping was death.

That helps us understand the saying, "He who would save his life will lose it, but he who loses his life will keep it." We have seen how the cynics of the early First Century C.E. comported themselves, *i.e.*, with little but the absolute necessities. Jesus went them one better and instructed his emissaries to carry not even a knapsack or extra pair of sandals. Could these have been the ones to whom Jesus might have said, "Give your one shirt as well as your one coat"? If so, the connection with losing and keeping becomes clearer. The one who would be a serious and intentional follower of Jesus embraces poverty so that he may have just enough to give away but not so much that he is bogged down by it. But if any of this is to make sense, the example must evolve into practice by a larger group of persons. It assumes that the principalities and powers have a major stake in a supplicant poverty class (cheap and compliant labor?) and a complete lack of understanding of those who are destitute, so far is the experience of the "haves" from the "have nots." In other words, the only help for the destitute will need to come from the merely poor whose poverty renders them able to appreciate destitution as being only a day or two away.

The merely poor were evidently able to eke out a living of some kind if only through conscripted labor. So while today they may have only one shirt and one coat apiece, they may be able to earn enough tomorrow or next week to buy one more of each ... to give away. These are tough terms, and they astound people who can afford the money to buy books like these and who have the time to read them. These terms would not appeal to the evangelist who is trying to attract new church members – at least not from among the American middle class. But the terms make clearer what liberation theologians have been saying for a long time, *viz.*, that Jesus was/is on the side of the poor and destitute. Indeed, Crossan's "thin line between poverty and destitution" is where he figures Jesus concentrated his presence and social commentary.

What judgment that implies for the church and for Christianity in general which are so totally identified with imperium! On a recent visit to Rome, I experienced anew the tremendous temporal power of the church. I stood in the vast nave of a basilica and looked at its columns and remembered that Constantine the Great had them erected there, having taken them from the Roman Forum where they had represented the power of pagan imperium. Now they represent the power of Christian imperium. I wondered how, credibly, a sermon on "give your one shirt as well as your one coat" could ever have been preached from the pulpit of that church.

Where to go with this troubling saying? Back to the drawing board with the whole of the Christian movement to see how and where and why it became identified with economic, military and political power – how it got itself co-opted by the principalities. This church of ours has drawers and drawers full of shirts (Jay Gatsby?) And closets full of coats. It is in uneasy partnership in most places in the developed world with the power structure. How can it recover the blessed poverty it must embrace in order to permit it fairly to embrace the Name of Jesus?

36

## Forgive seventy times seven

True to form, this saying has long since been laid claim to by a church interested in personal, emotional hurts inflicted on individuals by other individuals. "Sinning against" a person has come to mean doing him or her an injury that can be atoned for by sincere verbal apology and contrition. True, such transgressions are de-humanizing and are certainly a proper concern for followers of Jesus. But the saying is linked in the gospel to – guess what? Once again to the economy. It is connected to economic debt and the necessity of its forgiveness by creditors when it becomes burdensome and counterproductive to the debtor. Debt is an advantage to the creditor and a disadvantage to the debtor – mostly unfair.

St. Paul had it right when he told the Christians in Rome that they should owe nothing to each other but mutual love (Romans 13:8).

Whence debt in the first place? It comes about because one party has more capital than he can use at a given moment and finds it a profitable bargain to lend some of it to one who is, for one reason or another, short of capital. Ranging from generally to inevitably, the motivation is profit from interest. It is no accident that one of the most potentially profitable sources of a bank's earnings is its credit card business. That 18% A.P.R., payed out like the hangman's rope to the capital-less to enable them to claim a sliver of the economic pie, is pure gravy to creditors. In obvious concert with the advertising industry, the role of which is to appeal to and entice the capital-less with the glitz of having, the credit card companies lend capital with one hand and make it back in interest with the other. There is no countenance of forgiveness of any of that debt except through bankruptcy, access to which bank lobbyists are even now trying to foreclose.

Were these words to be read in the editorial suite of the Wall Street Journal, a bloodcurdling scream of outrage would be heard: First of all, he who dances must pay the fiddler. Second of all, money is property, and the Bible clearly enshrines private property rights, so debtors who do not or cannot repay borrowed capital are thieves, etc., etc. No forgiveness here.

Much earnest discussion obtained in the church during the year 2000 with regard to what is called "The Year of Jubilee." Following the biblical mandate of the jubilee, some church bodies are lobbying national and international agencies to forgive burdensome Third World debt even the interest on which some nations could never pay, much less could they repay principal. Somewhere in every discussion of that prospect will be heard a voice of beguiling reason patiently explaining that much Third World debt is held by financial institutions owned or invested in by citizens whose income derives from interest and principal repayment. To forgive Third World debt, besides being unsavory in the extreme (says that voice of reason), would be to deprive rightful owners of their full and deserved income, and would, furthermore, wreak havoc in the international financial markets.

That is probably true, but it would not have to be true. If the be all and end all of life is money and the security it affords, then there would certainly be trouble. If the attitude and belief is that capital is private property and not some pool of resources owned in condominium by all people, then what the editorial Cassandras at the Wall Street Journal gravely predict would almost surely come to pass. What Jesus apparently believed, though, is that capital is a resource that serves ends beyond itself and its having, therefore forgiveness of good faith debt in times and situations of compelling need might become an actualization of the kingdom (or rule) of God. Depend on the Jesus of the gospels to see salvation in economic terms. In that respect, he stands in the tradition of some of the prophets who were before him, perhaps Amos chief among them who called for "justice to roll down like waters and righteousness as an ever-flowing stream."

## Love your neighbor

On the face of it, this saying is uncomplicated. The verb conveys the Greek understanding of self-giving rather than possessive, possessing love. To that person who is neighbor to you, you are to demonstrate a non-possessive attitude, seeking to serve his or her needs, if not ahead of your own, at least not in competition with your own. He or she is expected to do the same. The results inherent in such an arrangement are obvious and desirable. There are, however, two problems: a) the people in with whom one is thrown in life are not necessarily lovable or inclined to find the reciprocation of unmerited kindness a natural response. Even members of one's nuclear family can at times be unlovable; b) basic human instinct calls for basic human beings to take care of themselves and their basic needs first – and maybe also last and always. Excepting maternal and sometimes even paternal instinct, we are a pretty self-centered lot. And at one level it's probably a good thing. In order to lose one's life in the gospel sense of the word, one must have a life in the first place. "Love your neighbor" is not an injunction against reasonable self preservation.

The real trouble with this saying presents itself when we press the issue of "who is my neighbor?" In most eras of human development, like folk have gathered by sect, clan, kith and kin. The homogeneous American suburbs, the gated communities, the country clubs and bowling leagues, the "truly growing"churches, which are the toast of evangelical Christianity, are all homogeneous by design. That is part of their success. So, at least to some degree, one can choose his or her neighbors. But if you pose the question of the identity of your neighbor within earshot of the third evangelist, Luke, you get far more than you bargained for. Luke attached a midrash to the straightforward, three-word saying, "Love your neighbor."

"A man was going down from Jerusalem to Jericho and fell among thieves who robbed him and beat him and left him for dead ..." Try to imagine being the one who heard that story first. It would be akin to hearing Hamlet's soliloquy or Mozart's Jupiter Symphony for the first time. It would blow you away – especially if you were a Judean. The great hero of the story that begins on the treacherous descent from Jerusalem to Jericho is a Samaritan – "the Good Samaritan," as he is called by tradition. What he does in response to being confronted by the man beaten and robbed is what makes both the unnamed victim and the unnamed Samaritan neighbors and the venue in which the latter events on the road took place a neighborhood. So one's neighbor is either a) the person in need or b) the person who has the means to meet that need, and a neighborhood becomes the place in which the need is met and, therefore, neighbors are made.

Loving your neighbor, then, does not necessarily mean loving those who live next door (though that is, of course, desirable and contributes to the cause of peace and the general welfare). Loving one's neighbor is not a casual act or general disposition – though being generally disposed to such love is also desirable. The love of neighbor is like the fire engine in the firehouse – always ready to move out to deal with what needs to be done. It is an ever-present awareness and willingness to help. It is a vocation that may supersede anything else when push comes to shove. It is a willingness in readiness that was modeled by the Samaritan of Luke's fertile novelist's imagination. Luke no doubt chose to make the protagonist of his matchless story a Samaritan to make it crystal-clear that "neighbor" for him and for Jesus did not necessarily mean a person "just like you." Judeans and Samaritans considered each other to be beyond the pale. That's what that colloquy in John chapter 4 is all about. It matters not in the end whether it is on Mt. Gerizim or on Mt. Zion that one worships, or anywhere for that matter, but the spirit and the truth of a thing. Where neighbors are concerned, the spirit is a gladly giving one, and the truth of it all is in the positive exchange between the need and the resource.

## Love your enemy

Now that we know something about who our neighbor is, we can deduce the sense of who the enemy might be. If we are to love him, her or them in the same sense of the verb by which we are called to love neighbor, then the enemy is not going to be substantively different from the neighbor, *i.e.*, another human being with similar basic urges, necessities and aspirations as you or I – setting aside for the moment the perversion of a psychopath or sociopath. An enemy in common parlance is one who wants what you are or have or believe you have the right to possess, and identifies him/her self by acting to take it from you. The centurion who ordered the peasant Judean or Galilean to carry his soldier's gear for one mile is the enemy because the "lawful" order is an attempt to rob the peasant of his/her dignity. We have already seen how one can preserve that dignity, not by refusal to carry out the order but by voluntarily "walking the second mile." If it is possible to perform that voluntary act with grace, it could be said that it was an act of love (agape). The one who summons the strength and grace to turn the other cheek after being struck on the first, if not outright loving the enemy who has done the terrible thing, has at least not multiplied the violence. Thus "loving" the enemy may be more a case of contributing to a culture of non-violence and forbearance than a one-on-one exchange.

This becomes more difficult when the enemy is writ large as in a Hitler or a Saddam Hussein. Did those, including Dietrich Bonhoeffer, who plotted to assassinate Adolf Hitler, contribute to peace or to its opposite? It is silly on the face of it to tell members of an American middle class congregation that they must love Saddam Hussein, for there is no practical or effective way to do so. Perhaps then, loving the enemy in a macro-sense becomes a matter of general attitude and disposition – quite opposite of the particularity of loving neighbor.

Then there is the one-on-one exchange between perceived enemies that may speak both to particularity and generality. An unforgettable passage in Harper Lee's 1960 American classic **To Kill a Mockingbird** depicts Jean Louise (Scout) Finch, eight-year-old daughter of Atticus Finch, disarming a lynch mob intent upon hanging Tom Robinson, Atticus' African-American client who was alleged to have raped a 19-year-old white woman – despite the fact the whole town knew that the woman had been the sexual aggressor and had been beaten senseless by her redneck father who witnessed his daughter's actions. When Scout spots Walter Cunningham, the father of one of her schoolmates, in the lynch mob, she engages him in conversation, mentioning her young friend and so defuses what might have been a bloody confrontation if the mob had attempted to seize Tom and, in so doing, would have shot and maybe killed Atticus. Scout's unlikely conversation with Walter Cunningham made him see that Atticus Finch, his perceived adversary, was a parent just as he was. And that altered the chemistry of the stand-off. It was Walter Cunningham who called off the lynching and caused the mob to disperse.

In the moments before the mob's dispersal, Scout Finch and Walter Cunningham were enemies. Scout, the one at severe disadvantage, a child unarmed and caring only that her father was not harmed, was the one who turned an enemy, if not into a friend, at least into one who laid down his arms and persuaded others to do so. Thus did Scout reach out to one individual as a fellow human being and appealed to him as one child to one parent, but in so doing contributed in a macro-sense to the prevention of violence.

That is a classic case of loving the enemy. She didn't shower him with hugs and kisses. She didn't say she liked him or wanted to marry his son. She just reached out, albeit in desperation, across the abyss of misunderstanding that more often than not separates even well-meaning people and managed to connect. It is when such an opportunity presents itself that one who has in readiness the willingness and the courage to act can and does, in fact, act that the end of the commandment to love the enemy is realized.

## Do to others what you would have done to yourself

Although nowhere in the gospel texts is it indicated as such, it seems reasonable to observe that the so-called Golden

Rule serves as a kind of summary of the content of the Jesus sayings. Hillel put it in the negative ("What you would not have done to you, do not do to another") which helps one more clearly appreciate the effect of the idea. If a significant number of persons really took this saying seriously and could find the emotional and mental wherewithal to apply it consistently, the state of the world would become far different than it is. Jesus evidently believed that human beings had it within them to be thus disposed. It was central to the wisdom the human being possessed ("the kingdom of God is within you" would be one metaphorical way of stating it). What is not said, but, I think, implied, is that one needs to live life not in a calculated fashion in which one schemes to erect a *quid pro quo* for every last thing. In other words, I do not love you so that you will love me. But I love you because I love you, and if you respond in kind, then, Jesus would say, the kingdom (the rule) of God has been realized. If not, it is there in potential.

That seems on the face of it to be asking the well-nigh impossible of human beings who are, after all, human. But it seems clearer and clearer as a result of contemporary scholarship that Jesus' ethical corpus offers a different version of "being human." Being human or "only human" does not necessarily mean being less than the ideal as a matter of course. It can mean being truly human which is the keeping and fulfillment of the seven sayings. It's what Paul may have meant in his own Neo-Platonic way about living after the spirit. To turn the other cheek, etc., is not to be superhuman but just plain human. It can be the rule rather than the exception. It does not take some intervention from outside the human experience to make it so. We are able.

Such a statement flies in the face of generations of Christian theology in which the human being is seen as totally depraved and without means to attain any level of worth. It flies in the face of Lutheran theology and of the epoch-making observations of Augustine. The late Karl Barth would insist that, on his/her own, the human being is out of luck. Paul scoffed at human wisdom as able to lead one anywhere except to a dead end. But that was not what Jesus seemed to be saying. If, indeed, he ever did utter anything akin to "the rule of God is within you," then from several of the other sayings reasonably attributed to him it is obvious that he – or whoever crafted those sayings – believed that human beings do have what it takes to make a just and peaceful society.

What has so badly obscured the validity of that proposition is the idea that "salvation" has to do with some time or place other than here and now. The outright abduction of the historical Jesus and his ethical wisdom teachings by theologians of the imperium who would make "salvation" into the stuff of mythology and connect it to some future, other life beyond death has to be acknowledged.

Jesus was talking about here and about now. The kingdom or rule of God was not, in the mind of the one who gave us the seven sayings around which this book is built, a thing of the apocalypse or end-times. It was this life that he was living then and that we are living now, and no other. That's what makes Jesus so much a person of this present age.

ChapterThree

# Jesus For Today

The last thing I want this book to do is to convince any-
body that Jesus is a – or worse, the – "Son of God." For
one thing, that language is meaningless. "God" is a se-
mantic projection of human surmise upon a vast and largely
unknown universe. The word "god" in no way can be said to
account for anything that is verifiable. Yet, natural phenomena
viewed in a certain way suggest that behind their existence
may be a benign intelligence of some considerable power and
purpose. But the insistence that one person in the whole course
of the human epoch in one nanosecond of cosmic time is some-
how the exclusive, deliberately appointed offspring of that intelligence is a leap so high over an abyss so deep requiring so
much willing abandonment of reason and common sense that

it must be resisted. It must be resisted especially when it becomes a driving force for political, economic, or military agenda. That the reigning Caesar was "God" was one of the driving forces behind the Roman expansion and hegemony in Galilee and Judea – among other places – in the first third of the First Century C.E. What became Christianity through first having been a branch of Judaism arose in opposition to Rome and to help the Palestinian peasant class cope with economic depredations. Sooner than one could possibly wish, Christianity began to take on the characteristics of the very thing that brought it into existence.

By the early Second Century, the long march toward theocracy had begun. It culminated in the Constantinian age of realized Christian imperialism in which people were executed not for their wretched treatment of the poor or for any infraction of what Jesus taught about how human beings could best treat one another, but because they could not or would not, for example, confess belief in Jesus as God. Whole cities and populaces fought in the streets over whose received revelation from on high was the one that conveyed the truth. That could not have been what the Jesus of the seven sayings had in mind. Even Matthew (Chapter 4) depicted Jesus resisting imperium.

Thus it is no claim for Jesus' exclusive divinity that makes him a person for this age or any age, this season or all seasons. It is the wisdom of the ethos explicated in those seven sayings and in more that can be reasonably attributed to him.

To make Jesus fairly and effectively known and accessible to this time and place (North America at the dawn of the 21st Century C.E.), his exponents need to take two measures: 1) Make clear that their "story" – its traditional liturgies and theologies with their pre-Enlightenment language and concepts (often triumphal and imperial in nature) – is an imperfect metaphorical vehicle transporting the truth – such as it can be known – about the person and ethos of Jesus from one time and circumstance to another, but not that truth itself; 2) Reform the church, which is inextricably bound up with his name, in ways that make it credible as a teacher and preacher of the content of the seven sayings. It does the cause no good to have rival sects and denominations within it each claiming to be the "thing itself" and making claims of exclusive franchise for salvific efficacy.

At the moment, the most obvious evangelical efforts of contemporary American Christianity consist of rallies, preaching missions, revivals, cult-like youth movements (e.g., Teen

Mania and Acquire the Fire) which hold up Jesus as a kind of larger-than-life figure who can be "loved" and "followed" much as one would a matinee idol. The focus is on "salvation," on being saved that the saved one may be guaranteed eternal life with God which Jesus purchased with his bloody sacrifice on the cross. – I shudder to write those last words.

Matinee idols come and go, and so will the Jesus of the Promise Keepers and the emotion-driven rallies. Between the first infatuation and the inevitable ennui, nothing much of the humanist ethic gets worked out or worked on. That is because Jesus is sold as a commodity for personal consumption rather than being presented as a teacher of an ethic that could, in fact, save the world from itself.

That is why, after the elitist reactions to my children's WWJD camp bracelets, I readily admitted that such guidance in the application of the seven sayings in effective and credible ways is what can save Christianity (and maybe the church) from irrelevance.

One need only pick up a decent newspaper or watch a television news program to grasp the fact that human beings continue to make a mess out of their world. Start anywhere. Start with environmental degradation, the destruction of the ozone layer, the profit-driven emission of greenhouse gases, etc., etc. Proceed to Kosovo or the Sudan, to Iraq and Iran and to wherever it is that human beings are oppressed, injured or killed as part of political, economic or religious agenda. One need not look far. At micro- and macro-levels, those seven sayings of Jesus can be taught both by precept and example. And in due course they will work. They need not – probably should not – be taught as part of a theological system but as what they appeared to be in the first place: everyday wisdom for living. Gandhi the Hindu embraced much of what he saw to be the ethic of Jesus without hauling along the entire theological imperium. The dream of the late Martin Luther King was based not on a fabricated theological idea of Jesus as an incarnate god or the god of the Jewish-Christian scriptures being the entire knowable reality of the divine, but on the simple precepts of the prophets and the sayings of Jesus.

Just as those prophets and that Jesus drove the philosophical impetus of the civil rights movement of the 1950s and 1960s, so they can drive any movement with peace and justice as its goals. What good is a heaven beyond time if time itself is not redeemed? Of all the various theologies Christendom has produced, perhaps liberation theology comes closest to what it's all about. Considerable resistance has been mounted against liberation theologians and their followers because their understanding of Jesus is as an exemplar and exponent of human freedom which can only be known, of course, in a community that values justice, equity and respect for the dignity of every human being. The interests vested in economic, social, and political hegemony naturally resist the Jesus of the liberators.

All the more reason that Christians of the 21st Century should lift him up by way of relearning his basic teachings, learning how to communicate them credibly as an ethical system and living them out in daily practice. Whatever else of Christendom goes by the board will be of no permanent loss, and some of it – especially the triumphalist, imperialist part – good riddance. Jesus can be the figure of an ethical revival that could go a long way toward the salvation of the world, but in far different terms than most Christians have ever envisioned.

Chapter Four

# How the Jesus Ethic Has Worked

I t is not as if the ethic of the seven sayings has not been tried successfully. It has in the lives of people to whom I have been a pastor and friend along the way. I do not mean that anyone I have ever known carried, phylactery-like, the seven sayings on his/her person and went about seeing how they might apply them one by one. I mean that a good many people I have known and admired – as many religiously non-aligned persons as not – have at telling passages in their lives acted and chosen in general, even specific ways, in accordance with the broad ethic of the seven sayings. This chapter will narrate some of that history without breaking pastoral or personal confidence. Names, places and other means of identifying actual situations have been carefully guarded, yet it is hoped that each reader will be able readily to identify with each incident or series of events.

## Roger and No. 44

It is an athletic contest in which two rival teams are competing for the conference championship. Roger, the star runner of his team, is perhaps six feet ahead of his closest competitor, who is wearing No. 44 on his jersey. As the competitor closes the distance and comes even with Roger, a bystander kicks a stone into the path of the competitor on which he trips and begins to fall. Roger reaches out to pull him back on track and ends up losing the race by a foot. The extraordinary incident took place just out of the sight of a stadium full of spectators who only saw that Roger had not won. Roger joined in the applause for his rival and left the field. A college chaplain, as it happened, had witnessed the incident of Roger aiding his rival and went immediately to the locker room to speak with him. Roger begged the chaplain not to tell anyone of the incident and to let it be. Roger's words were: "I would have expected him to do the same for me." The chaplain, perplexed, retorted, "You know perfectly well he wouldn't have." "Well, then that's his problem," Roger replied. "But what about your team?" said the chaplain. "They all lost because of your decision, which I grant was noble and right. Don't they deserve to know why they lost?" Roger shrugged and smiled, saying, "If they each ran their best, they didn't lose a thing." The chaplain was left with his jaw on his breast bone, speechless in the face of grace. "Do to others as you would have them do to you."

## The kindly banker and Eugene

Eugene was a war veteran who even as a lad had aspirations and ideas that seemed to be beyond the scope of his abilities. But he was as likable a fellow as one could ever hope to meet. When he returned from war one rank above the one at which he entered (buck private), he decided to try his hand as an insurance agent. The president (cashier and chief teller) of the small-town bank backed him with some capital. But Eugene sold policies to friends and neighbors and did battle with his underwriters to pay every claim. Soon the underwriters wrote him off, leaving him in debt to the bank. Next Eugene studied to become a real estate salesman, again with a loan from the local bank, or so he thought. Because Eugene was never content to hide any drawbacks or defects of the houses he was trying to sell, he sold few, and then often gave up parts of commissions because he could see how much his buyers were stretching to afford the most modest homes. Predictably enough, his career in real estate soon came to an end – and his debt greater. Eugene then found an opportunity to work toward a Dairy Queen franchise. The job seemed made for him because of his general friendliness and likability. He willingly employed a few of the town's teenagers who took dreadful advantage of him to the point that Dairy Queen rescinded its provisional franchise, and Eugene was again a man in search of a livelihood. By this time, the young clergyman in town had come to know Eugene who had come to him for advice. Eugene's debt was now severe, and he was having trouble paying even the interest. So the young pastor went to the banker to intercede. What he discovered was that, after the insurance debacle, the kindly banker had been lending Eugene funds out of his own personal reserves, being unwilling to encumber the bank with bad debt. "Somebody needs to believe in Eugene," the banker said. When Eugene fell seriously and, as it turned out, terminally ill, the kindly banker quietly tore up the promissory notes he had had Eugene sign over the years. "I wanted him to die free of debt," the banker said. And so he did.

## Armani and rags

A priest and one of his parishioners were walking along a sidewalk of a busy street in a city to which both had come for an important meeting. The priest wore his dark-suit-and-collar-backwards garb. The layman, a wealthy financier, wore one of his 50 or 60 tailored suits. They must have made a fine picture of the "Church Militant Here in Earth." A street person, an elderly appearing woman dressed in the tatters of what had once been a respectable dress, was sitting on the sidewalk with her back to the facade of a building. She was not begging but quietly weeping. The layman stopped dead in his tracks, approached the woman and said, "Mother, what's the matter? Do you need help?" The priest was both astonished and embarrassed – astonished because his impeccably clad companion had knelt on the sidewalk at the side of a filthy street person and embarrassed because he himself had not thought to do so first. The woman told the layman something to the effect that her poverty had cost her custody of her children to a social service agency, that their fathers had long abandoned them and her, and that she had only a sixth-grade education and slim prospects of a job.

The priest glanced surreptitiously at his watch, impatient to get to the important meeting for which he and his companion had come. But the latter had gone to a nearby pay telephone and, as it turned out, was speaking with a manager of the local branch of his firm, instructing him to come with a car so the woman could be taken to a church-run shelter and be fed, decently clothed and housed while case workers at the agency tried to find her a job, reunite her with her children and find them a home.

The layman instructed his branch manager to cut a check to the church-run shelter for such and such an amount to cover whatever costs would be entailed. The end of the story is that the financier followed up on the matter once he had returned home to the main office, and arranged for his general counsel to take up *pro bono publico* the matter of restoring custody of the children to their mother.

When the priest finally got an opportunity to speak with his companion about the incident and covered him with praise, the layman looked surprised and annoyed. "What do you think? I don't listen to you when you preach?" the latter asked. "Just three weeks ago you preached on the Good Samaritan. It was a moving sermon, and I remembered it instantly when I saw the poor woman. We just couldn't have walked on by."

The priest and his lay companion missed their important meeting. Or did they?

## The Late Robert and Why He Died

The mid-1960s were touchy times for America with the country divided over Vietnam. For some clergy, it meant heart-wrenching funerals for 18-year-old men/children on whose high school diplomas the ink was barely dry before their parents found a military officer at the front door bearing the evil tidings. Robert was one of the men/children who did not return from Vietnam. Only what was left of his body in a flag-draped coffin. The circumstances surrounding his death and funeral are painful to write about even 35 years later. Robert, so said his immediate superior officer, came upon a wounded Viet Cong guerrilla during a routine patrol. Orders were to shoot to kill before one was shot. But Robert's heart would not let him pull the trigger. As he knelt to ascertain whether the guerrilla was dead, a Viet Cong sniper blew the top third of his body into countless pieces of tissue and bone. The incident gave away the whereabouts of the American patrol, and it came under terrific fire. Understandably, Robert did not receive a commendation for his last act, it having been dereliction of duty.

The priest who celebrated his funeral mass gave a homily based on the text, "Love your enemy." The priest told the congregation that Robert had submitted himself to a higher authority in stooping perhaps to give comfort to his sworn enemy. Based on what the priest knew of Robert, he said to the congregation that it was probably second nature to Robert to care about another injured human being despite his enemy status. "In the midst of our sorrow, our anger and our frustration, we cannot fail to celebrate and give thanks for the final act of Robert's life," the priest said in his homily. "If only for a moment it appears that Robert loved his enemy, or, at the least, did not hate him. He may not have been the good soldier some of you may have wanted him to be that day, but he remembered what he had learned at home and church. Let him who is without ambiguity about the sometimes conflicting demands of God and country cast the first stone."

One local cemetery refused burial for Robert's body. The priest's church was picketed by veterans' groups the next Sunday causing one of the his colleagues to observe that "loving one's enemy, or even just talking about loving the enemy only makes you more enemies. This is the Good News of our Lord Jesus Christ?"

## Attention Deficit Disorder and Miss Trevelan

Teaching any grade in a fundamentally deprived school system in a city to whom the decades have not been kind can be a purgatory-like experience. Just ask Marlena Trevelan (not her real name). Ms. Trevelan is a distinguished graduate of a distinguished college who is serving a provisional internship-like term as a team teacher. She is required by contract to give an extra 40 minutes at the end of the day to provide special attention to low academic achievers who are obviously Attention Deficit Disorder kids. The teacher's collective bargaining unit made this concession for interns. The extra 40 minutes is derisively termed "combat" or "latrine" duty. Marlena finds it all that and more in her first couple of weeks. All her efforts seem to meet with indifference at best and open hostility at worst. She remarks to the pastor of the church she had recently joined that she would not have believed that fourth graders could be so menacing. As Thanksgiving approaches Marlena begins to notice a change in one or two of her students. They actually begin to respond to her efforts to help them. By Christmas, one of them, a nine-year-old boy, has made such progress that he is surpassing some of his classmates who had been doing quite well. Marlena warms to her work as she had not since September. Increasingly, the nine-year-old boy, followed by others, begins to blossom under her tutorial care. With the grudging permission of her principal and supervising teacher, she devises a half-hour before-school tutorial session. Soon she is dipping into her meager pay to bring fresh fruit for the children's breakfast, as she suspects some of them are undernourished. Burdened with the repayment of student loans, Marlena's daily purchase at the neighborhood fruit stand begin to make a negative impact on her cash flow.

By the end of the third marking period, Marlena's formerly troubled fourth-graders (the ones who voluntarily come early) are getting a new lease on their academic lives. For her trouble, she begins to be criticized – at first in whispers and later openly – by the school's veteran faculty. They resent her example as it evidently showed them what a little effort beyond the basic requirements could accomplish. During the semester break, the head of the local teachers' union files a grievance with the board of education and, without any input from her, Marlena's pre-school tutorials are stopped.

She goes to her pastor because she doesn't know where else to go and shares her anger and frustration. The priest agrees to try to get his parish council to approve the use of a room for an early morning breakfast program and Marlena's tutorial. With some difficulty the pastor is able to obtain agreement for a trial plan but informs Marlena that the parish would advance no funds for food or materials. Undaunted, Marlena goes ahead with her plans and digs even more deeply into her slender pocketbook to fund her work.

The end of the story is that eventually the parish could see the positive results of Marlena's efforts – especially the parents of some of the children involved who actually began to attend church and put money in the collection plate. By year's end, Marlena had quit her job with the school district, moved out of her apartment into the former sexton's quarters in the church's parish house, and begun work at a sinful hourly rate as the church's janitor. The joy of her life was her breakfast-tutorial program for neighborhood children, especially the after-school session added later as the teachers' union managed to kill the school's program by negotiating out of their contract the 40-minute after-school requirement. In the second year of Marlena's program, it expanded into Saturdays with full funding by the parish assisted by the diocese. A thoughtful lay person in the parish who early on became

an admirer of Marlena and a supporter of the program suggested a name for it which stuck for as long as it lasted: "The
Second Mile." Most people thought the name referred to the
extra effort the children made – or were required by their
parents to make. But I think it referred to something and someone else.

## Down at the Soup Kitchen

The congregation I serve as pastor takes its annual turn
among the parishes of the diocese each Palm Sunday in run-
ning a soup kitchen in Detroit's central city, which serves the
only hot meal available to indigents on Sunday – all other
meal providers being closed. Each year I have participated,
we have made and served 75 gallons of soup and more than
1,000 sandwiches to 500 to 800 persons. It is not more than a
15-minute, 10-mile drive from my suburban parish to the soup
kitchen. The journey, however, is from privilege to depriva-
tion. It is good for us to be reminded, if only once a year, of
the terrible disparity between our lives and those of our guests
for a day. What we see over a six-hour period is usually so-
bering and sad. But several Palm Sundays ago, I drew what is
known as "door duty," aiding guests as they enter the serving

area. That put me in close contact with each of the several hundred people who came, and within sight of the line forming outside.

On that Sunday some years back, I observed the following scene: A man I reckoned to be about 25 or 30 years old was standing at the end of the line when a woman carrying an infant came up behind him. Easter fell quite early that year, so Palm Sunday was in the third week of March, and it was typically cold and blustery. Rain mixed with snow was falling. I had observed over my years of participation in the soup kitchen project that there is often not much love lost between and among the guests who are already resentful of having to take charity to silence their growling stomachs. I had seen fights break out.

The young man I mentioned turned slightly as the infant-bearing woman got into line behind him. They seemed to exchange no words, but it was difficult not to notice that she had taken her own tattered jacket and wrapped it around her baby, leaving her shivering in a second-hand man's shirt as the rain fell upon them. The young man began to exhibit signs of agitation and seemed to be talking to himself. He grimaced at no one in particular and stamped his feet as if to

69

stimulate circulation. I think the baby must have been crying because the woman seemed anxious as cradle-like she rocked her arms back and forth. This went on for some minutes as the line snailed its way forward. Then suddenly the young man pulled off his own jacket, then an old sweatshirt with the faded monogram of some college or university. I saw him speak briefly to the woman as he held both arms out. Yes, she was handing him the baby, then putting his sweatshirt on her own body. He would not give the baby back until she apparently agreed also to put on his jacket as he now stood jacketless in the rain. Through the window I saw someone in line come into view bearing a much-dented garbage can lid which he attempted to hold as an umbrella over  the young woman with the baby. I became aware that a tear was making its way down one of my cheeks, and I asked to be relieved of my post for a moment to compose myself. I had earlier that morning cheered on the 50 or so volunteers from my congregation who were giving up their Sunday – some of them had also given a good portion of Saturday to help prepare the soup ingredients – to serve others according to the biblical mandate. How fatuous a homiletic gesture, I thought, for I had just witnessed one important biblical mandate being acted upon at the level on which Jesus must have talked about the shirt and the coat.

As the line worked its way forward, I never did see the man who had given away his (only?) coat and (only?) shirt. I asked the guard who was my counterpart outside what might have happened to him. The guard, who worked at the soup kitchen every Sunday, said the man had finally sought shelter from the rain and probably would not reappear to get his meal. When the young woman finally appeared inside she still held her baby with one hand and arm and **two** tickets in the other hand. Did the man who gave up coat and shirt also give her his meal ticket?

Chapter Five

# The Human Potential in Secular Thought

D istinct echoes of the ethic of the seven sayings have resounded here and there in the thought of Western philosophers, and their work has by turns found its way into the manner by which democratic societies have tried to live.

Such minds as John Locke's figured out that a peaceful and secure way of life would have to be based on a sense of community. In his **Two Treatises on Civil Government**, Locke said a civil society came about when people agreed "to join and united into a community, for their comfortable, safe and peaceable living, one amongst another, in a secure enjoyment of their properties..."

It does not seem possible to conceive of the success of

such a society apart from a commitment to the kind of ethic with which we have been concerned. It does not diminish the individual but does put upon the individual the onus for making the system work. Garry Wills in his 1999 **A Necessary Evil** writes of the division of labor which is a requirement of such a system (p. 301). He reaches as far back as Plato's **Republic** for the argument which Plato places on the lips of Socrates. It is a familiar argument featuring a hypothetical farmer who has the choice between the self-sufficiency of supplying all his own needs, or of doing well what he does best and engaging the products of his industry in trade with those who perform other task yielding goods and services he cannot efficiently produce and provide. Such a system must have at its foundation such an ethic as outlined in the seven sayings. Clearly Locke, and before him Plato, believed the human being was equipped to make such a society work. A First Century C.E. sage might say, "The kingdom of God is within you."

Wills in the aforementioned work makes the case that government is more than "a necessary evil" but, in fact, a necessary good. In so saying, he quotes from David Hume (**A Treatise on Human Nature**) to the effect that human beings naturally desire community that can provide a sharing of necessities and the security in which to enjoy them, meagre as they might be.

Hume's 18th Century theories have resonated well with contemporary philosophers and psychologists. His "pain and pleasure" analysis of how the human being acts and reacts emphasizes the primacy of reason and its empirical bases. Hume locates integrity in a personal disposition that seeks harmony within itself and with society. Such harmony brings pleasure – so one discovers in the application of reason to available choices and the process of making them – and that pleasure cannot be at the expense of another's pain. This is, it is plain to see, another way of saying "as you would have done to you, do to others."

Hume went so far as to observe that whatever brings pleasure has what he called "utility," that is to say a condition or set of conditions that works for rather than against individual and common welfare. A thing, event or development cannot bring pleasure if it brings pain to anyone because the appreciation of utility – or what works – entails what he called "sympathy," in which another person's pain (or pleasure) becomes the other's as a result of which both parties become interested in the general welfare and seek a common good. This all works together, Hume observed, to produce a "moral sense" developed by the association of virtues to which utility speaks. Virtues, Hume would say, are good because of their utility; they would not be good (or virtues) if their existence and exercise did not contribute positively to the community's welfare.

Hume does not say that all virtues arise naturally. Indeed, he would say that beyond such "natural" impulses of parental love lie an array of impulses that arise out of the experience of trial and error – trial and error proving that utility (what works for the good of all concerned) is the goal. Nowhere does Hume say that the utility of ethics is beyond the reach of human beings. Everywhere in his analysis is implied the well-examined conviction that it is with the ability of human beings to seek and work for common "pleasure."

Before Hume came Thomas Hobbes of the 17th Century. Hobbes' ethical philosophy is founded on what he called the "natural right" the human being has to have or to do anything he pleases. Over against this he posited "natural law," a precept discovered through reason. One obeys that natural law, which challenges the natural right, for reasons of self-interest. Thus Hobbes' first and fundamental natural law is that human beings should seek peace, not as some discrete ideal but as a condition in which one can enjoy what he may, yet in concert with others who have the same natural right as he – all under the natural law. That is Hobbes' naturalistic interpretation of the Golden Rule. Thus the renunciation of unbridled claiming of the natural right is a mutual act under an accepted law effecting a social contract – of which human beings are capable.

Coming at it from the rationalistic rather than empirical point of view was Immanuel Kant (1724-1804). Kant said that all things knowable – even the laws of mathematics and physics – owe their origin to the structure of the human mind. No less ethics. Kant's famous "categorical imperative" is an *a priori* principle which should command human behavior rendering actual behavior inferior to that which the imperative mandates. "Oughtness," not is-ness" is what counted for Kant. It is within human capacity, due to the powers of reason, as he wrote in **The Critique of Practical Reason**, to treat every human being, including oneself, as an end in himself and not as a means to the advantage of anyone else. For Kant it was, as he famously said, "The starry heavens above and the moral law within." Society, government, religion – all are means by which the moral law within can be made operative in an individual's life. Again, for Kant, it is within the human being to be moral, to do what is right.

From the 17th and 18th Centuries to the 19th, we come to consider one of the most eloquent political texts in our national history. Within two months of his assassination at the hands of John Wilkes Booth, Abraham Lincoln at his second inauguration delivered what has been called the "purest gold of human eloquence": "With malice toward none; with charity for all; with firmness in the right, as God gives us to see the right, let us strive on to finish the work we are in; to bind up the nation's wounds; to care for him who shall have borne the battle, and for his widow and his orphan – to do all which may achieve and cherish a just and lasting peace among ourselves and with all nations."

Booth's bullet fixed it so Lincoln could not employ his ample political and moral capital in the binding up of the nation. One can only speculate at how much of the horrors of Reconstruction and their bitter fruit still being harvested well into the 20th Century might have been avoided by a complete second term for the Great Emancipator.

The vision of the peroration of the Second Inaugural set forth an astonishing agenda considering the political, social and historical culture in and to which it was uttered. Even at such a grim juncture, Lincoln, whom no one could sanely call a utopian, envisioned the healing of a nation, the mending of its rent fabric by the sheer will and intention of its brutalized population in which deep resentments made only deeper by half a decade of all-out war still festered. Lincoln clearly believed that healing could come to pass, that it was within the nation's people to effect it. He had already at Gettysburg connected the proposition that "all men are created equal" with the purpose for the War Between the States. At Gettysburg he memorably said that the struggle on that battlefield was not about the military superiority of North or South but the liberation of the slaves: "The world will little note nor long remember what we say here, but it can never forget what they did here. It is for us, the living, rather, to be dedicated to the unfinished work which they who fought here have thus far so nobly advanced." The new "birth of freedom" Lincoln envisioned, like "the work" he referenced in the Second Inaugural, had to do with how people treated other people, black and white. It was within slaves to forgive their

79

former owners, and within the former slave owners to appreciate their former slaves as ones created equal to them. To such a view, the seven sayings, the core of the ethic of Jesus, gives affirmation.

The potential is within us. But, of course, history does not seem to bear out this point. The whole apparatus of Christian neo-orthodoxy which descended upon the theological enterprise after World War I was essentially pessimistic. It took the monumental horror of the Great War as evidence that the whole liberal structure as erected by Locke, Hume, Kant and others was invalid. Neo-orthodoxy arrived on the brooding wings of biblicism and a rediscovery of the Pauline/Augustinian, essentially Platonic world of flesh and spirit. The ideological bottom line was, contrary to Milton's observations that human intellect can make a heaven of hell, that the human intellect can make only hell of heaven and more hell of hell. As Paul insisted in his put-down of human wisdom, "For God's foolishness is wiser than human wisdom" (I Corinthians 1:25a NRSV).

That dictum did not usher in any golden age of human endeavor and progress. Nor did Augustine's largely dim view of the human being's potential stem the tide of the Dark Ages.

All of which is to say that consigning the fate of the race to the mercies of an unseen and unknowable "god" who may or may not be disposed to salvific activity on our behalf is not a promising strategy. The scorning of human wisdom by those who profess belief in a god in whose image human beings supposedly have been made would seem thereby to scorn their god. Those who salivate over the depravity – total or otherwise – of humanity likewise call the mercies of their god into question.

Certainly it is valid to shake the head in dismay over the stupidity and occasional atrocities of what Robert Burns called "man's inhumanity to man." Just as among a representative pool of human beings there are psychopaths and sociopaths, just so in the course of history there are bound to be psychopathic and sociopathic events. But neither the horror of the Second World War nor the imbecility of the Korean or Vietnam conflicts diminishes the accomplishment of the United Nations' creation and six decades of history. Certainly the race seems often to take one step forward and two back. Often enough we seem to be a prisoner of Zeno's paradox in which we only seem to advance half the remaining distance toward perfection – meaning which, at that rate, we'll never arrive.

History and historians, though, only do journalism on a greater scale. Newspapers and broadcast news agencies seldom trumpet headlines about a normal, pleasant day having passed in Peoria. History constitutes the annals of struggle, of victory and defeat, of war and aftermath. Any school boy or girl will know what Dec. 7, 1941, and Aug. 6, 1945, signify. Neither date nor the event it memorializes represents the best of human endeavor. But many other dates of those years, despite the era, no doubt witnessed ordinary people treating other ordinary people with care, respect and dignity. Even at Pearl Harbor and Hiroshima were documented numerous acts of heroic mercy and sacrifice. Such acts do not erase the awful carnage of those events. They do not redeem them, but they do bear witness to the capacity of the human being to act selflessly.

Thus Locke, Hume, Hobbes and Kant with their Enlightenment views of humanity were not mistaken or gulled into a false optimism. It is within a person to do what the Jesus of the seven sayings would do, because such things are done countless times a day by countless persons, often enough unselfconsciously, because to do unto others what one would have done to the self is the ultimate pragmatism or, as Hume would say, utility.

# Conclusion

For far too long Christianity has been largely an institution of belief and ritual where correctness of thought and theology was primary. Orthodoxy – literally "being straight," as in "orthodontics" – has a long history of oppression and irrelevance, as if any human being could have the slightest workable clue about anything beyond what the senses can perceive and reason process. The church has divided, sometimes violently, over what should be believed about things beyond human experience but seldom over how human beings should be treated. At least 19th Century American Baptists and Methodists split over slavery, and pacifist groups have separated themselves from greater Christendom over opposition to bearing arms against other human beings.

Generally, though, it is belief, liturgical practice and polity that hold Christian groups together.

It is not clear how committed Jesus may actually have been to one particular strain of First Century Judaism over others. The gospel writers, variously, depict him in conflict with the Pharisees, Sadducees and – John observes – with "the Jews." From the exorcism in the Capernaum synagogue (Mark), to the proclamation of good tiding to the poor and captive in the Nazarene synagogue (Luke), to urging the voluntary second mile (Matthew/Luke) to the mandate of agape (John – "Love one another as I have loved you"), Jesus seemed to have been concerned with how people treated one another. The "kingdom of God" he claimed was in us is the wisdom and grace to treat others as we ourselves would be treated. What else could it be? And if it is something else or something more, it is certainly that to begin with. If it is necessary to connect this humanist ethic to some theological system, can we not be content to say that if there is some will of some superhuman intelligence and power for how human life forms on this planet can best treat one another, that will may be expressed to some degree in the seven sayings of Jesus with which we have been concerned? If it is necessary to posit that ethic's origin outside of the human experience to make it salable in the religious marketplace, then let the theologians have their day. But let them not get obsessed with orthodoxy, and by all means not make their work an end in itself but a means to the end of defending the ethic found in those seven sayings of Jesus as fundamental to the success of the human enterprise on Earth. Let the theologians join forces with the scholars of comparative religion to discover how similar to Jesus' ethic may be those of other religions and humanist traditions in other cultures and find ways to lift up all that for world-wide attention. It would not be the first time that religious activity and speculation had inspired human beings to treat each other, well, humanely.

According to Titus Livius (Livy) the Roman historian of antiquity, Numa, an 8th Century B.C.E. ruler of Rome, chose to use religion as a tool for civic improvement. "Rome had originally been founded by force of arms," Livy wrote in **The Early History of Rome** (1. 19-21), "the new King (Numa) now prepared to give the community a second beginning, this time on the solid basis of law and religious observance ... war, he well knew, was no civilizing influence, and the proud spirit of his people could be tamed if only they learned to lay aside their swords. ... By these means the whole population of Rome was given a great many new things to think about and to attend to, with the result that everybody was diverted from military preoccupations ... believing, as they now did, that the heavenly powers took part in human affairs..." (Translated by Aubrey DeSelincourt, Penguin Books, 1971)

If salvation is the principal concern of religion, it will never be the result of coerced belief in fabricated propositions veiled as received revelation. It will come, if it ever comes, if and when enough human beings make the choice to treat each other as they would be treated, to turn the other cheek, to walk the second mile, to love their neighbors and their enemies as neighbors, to give the shirt as well as the coat and to forgive as often as it takes.

If anything deserves to be called "the kingdom (or rule) of God," that is it. It would be a mistake to think that what is termed "the Jesus ethic" is complex and nuanced beyond the comprehension of all but the most erudite theologians or church hierarchs. It is simple, but not simplistic. It does not require more than consistent teaching by example and the quiet insistence and persistence of a committed core of intentional people. The only major challenge is to make, for example, the turning of the second cheek the rule rather than the exception. When it becomes the rule, fewer first cheeks will be smitten to begin with. The point will have been made. The slapping of the first cheek produces unwanted pain. And the long-term way of avoiding such pain is to keep turning the other cheek until cheeks are slapped no more. To repeat, none of this is rocket science or neurosurgery. It is not mystery-laden theory. It is simply a way of living that in the longer term is far more fulfilling for all concerned than the way we live now.

No intervention from on high is needed to effect the onset of that way of life. No vast upheaval of the world is required. It will not be found in an apocalypse. It will be found, as Jesus is quoted as saying, "within." We human beings have that power and potential. It is dishonest of us to consign the Jesus ethic to an unattainable utopia and to say, "Meanwhile, we're only human. But when the kingdom of God comes, things will be different." New Testament scholarship is more and more disclosing a Jesus who believed that the only so-called kingdom of God was already present in the minds and abilities of human beings, that the human race had within its grasp anything it needed to order its collective life in just and peaceful ways. From the Code of Hammurabi to the 613 commandments of Torah to the Bill of Rights of the U.S. Constitution to the International Declaration of Human Rights come *prima facie* evidence that Jesus was right.

The focus, then, has got to be on humanity and on individual human beings. It is from it and from them that "salvation" will come, if it will come at all. If it does, we will have ourselves to thank as well as whatever source of life and ordering wisdom set us upon the evolutionary path. If it does not, we will have ourselves to blame and, were there such a thing as a final tribunal, much to answer for in not having reached for anything near our full potential.

John Milton wrote, "The mind is its own place, and in itself, can make a heav'n of hell, a hell of heav'n." (Paradise Lost, Book One).

# Appendix

It is only fair for an author who proposes the kind of approach I have advocated in this little book to demonstrate how it can be successfully and – one would hope – effectively preached in the life of a working congregation. And thus are offered in this appendix two sermons that flow philosophically from this exposition. The first, entitled, "Saying Nothing Out of Fear," was given from the pulpit of St. Andrew's Episcopal Church in Clawson, Michigan, on Easter Sunday 2000. The second, which bears the title "Ovine vs. Divine," was preached three weeks later to the same congregation. Admittedly, in a purely theoretical sense, both sermons represent, at best, heterodoxy and, at worst, outright heresy. In a practical sense, though, both represent a working theological and pastoral hypothesis which plays out effectively in the life of a congregation of typical American Episcopalians who are only trying to do their best with what resources they have in being part of the solution rather than the problem.

## Sermon 1: "Saying Nothing Out of Fear"

The first people to have a clue that death might not have been the last word on Jesus told no one of their stupendous hunch because, according to Mark, they were afraid. But obviously they eventually told somebody because Mark knew the story. Something inexplicable convinced the very earliest of Jesus' associates that the Romans' execution of him had not silenced him for good. Perhaps they had day-dreams and night visions of his ghostly presence. Maybe they thought they heard him speaking to them. Who knows?

Some of the gospel writers got carried away and reported such incidents as if they had actually physically occurred. One of Christianity's most serious weaknesses has come in taking all of that sort of thing literally. What those stories say in the most graphic way possible is that even such a political and military colossus as Rome, such an entrenched tradition as Temple Judaism could not, separately or together, put Jesus down or keep him down. That's the Easter story.

He who advocated the equal love of neighbor and enemy, who counseled the passive resistance of turning the other cheek and walking the second mile, who championed the economy of giving the shirt as well as the coat and forgiving debtors seventy times seven was not to be buried in the obscurity of defeat. The ethic of doing to others what one would have done to self did not – does not – depend on the authority of government or the brute power of the military. No law can effectively command it, no array of weaponry, no threat of suppression can snuff it out. That's the Easter story.

It is an ethic for the ages and for The Age. It is the rule of God – as the scriptures would characterize it. It is the perfection of Adam and the blessed light of the New World. No one ever said it would be easy to proclaim that ethic, much less to live it out. It is hard. If it weren't hard, everybody would be doing it.

Certainly the first ones to appreciate the enduring presence of Jesus were afraid to tell of it. Why wouldn't they have been? The powers that spared no effort to kill him would certainly pursue his followers. But, of course, the followers eventually did speak up and out. The way they had learned from him worked - even though by its very nature it mocked the way the world worked.

He was killed because of that. He lives because he was right, and the world was wrong. And still is. It is a fearful thing to say that and to act it out. But that's why we're here today. We're here not to be told that everything is hunky-dory, that Jesus has just cut the ribbon to open a four-lane superhighway to heaven. We're here to be reminded that he died in the cause of right, and that his cause did not die with him. We're here to be reminded that our baptisms drafted us into his cause, and that if we're not proclaiming, insisting on and living out his ethic, we are deserters.

The alleluias of Easter are more than hymnody; they are trumpet blasts calling us to oppose the malign might of the world's principalities and powers with the ethic of the Golden Rule. Do those trumpet blasts make you afraid? They do me. The first of those who heard them were afraid, too. The real Easter finally came on the day they found their voice.

So today is not Easter, or not necessarily. Tomorrow might be, if you and I and other Christians find our voices and raise them in protest of all the injustices that flow from those who treat others not as they themselves would be treated. Saying nothing out of fear does not get any stone rolled away from any grave.

## Sermon 2: "Ovine vs. Divine"

The word appears with some frequency in the New York Times crossword puzzle: "ovine" – o-v-i-n-e. It means sheep-like, just as "bovine" means cow-like, "porcine" means pig-like, "equine" means horse-like, "feline" cat-like, "canine" dog-like and "divine" god-like. Which one is your aspiration?

If you paid attention to the gospel reading today, you understand that the writer of the Gospel according to John likens you and me to sheep. The verb most often used in connection with sheep is "to herd." That's what you have to do with sheep: herd them. They need to be herded because they are of exceptionally low-grade intelligence if, indeed, it can be said that they have any intelligence at all.

The writer of John may have picked up the sheep-shepherd metaphor from the piece of poetry we call "the 23rd Psalm," that dearly beloved text that has brought so much comfort to so many for so long. And I suppose it is comforting and comfortable to think of an unseen but benignly gentle shepherd guiding one's way through uncertainty or suffering or approaching death. But after that, the metaphor loses its grip, because human beings who want to be responsible and in control are most definitely not sheep desirous of being herded. I've hardly ever known an Episcopalian who wanted to be herded.

Oh, we love to see our bishops decked out in cope and miter carrying their shepherd's crook, but god help them if they try to prod us with the bottom or pull us along with the top.

And that's OK, because we're closer to being divine than we are to being ovine. My next book which has a tentative title "Ethics 101 – What Would Jesus Do?" presumes that Jesus was fully human, that he knew every frailty and every weakness that we know, that he struggled as we struggle and that the leadership under him to which we submit ourselves is as to an older, wiser sibling. Jesus, then, is a teacher and mentor, not a shepherd – and we are not sheep.

One of the remarkable comments put on Jesus' lips by the author of Matthew's gospel is: "Be ye therefore perfect as your Father in heaven is perfect" – and unless someone is taunting us, we can assume from that remark that divinity is within our grasp, or, more to the point, within us waiting to come out.

It seems reasonable to think that if there stands behind us and all existence a purposeful intelligence – and that is generally part of the Jewish-Christian belief system – then it is reasonable to believe that that intelligence which may have given us life and purpose has imprinted itself upon us. The majestic procession of the evolution of biological life from unicellular forms to what we are and who we as human beings strongly suggests that divinity may be another way of accounting for humanity. But, you would counter, humanity is flawed, imperfect – messed up, even. And you'd be right. Perhaps that saying from Matthew is better translated "**become** perfect as your Father is heaven is perfect." The word we translate "perfect" is a Greek word meaning "finished, completed or fulfilled." So we can, as the saying goes, get there from here.

In any event we are not sheep or sheep-like. We are not ovine. And we are not static beings. We are in development and on the way to becoming something other than we are at present. I would therefore counsel that we reject the image and metaphor of sheep and shepherd, and seek to become divine rather than ovine.

# Bibliography

Borg, Marcus J., **Jesus, A New Vision**, 1987, SPCK

Borg, Marcus J., **Jesus In Contemporary Scholarship**, 1994, Valley Forge

Borg, Marcus J., and N.T. Wright, **The Meaning of Jesus**, 1999, Harper San Francisco

Crossan, John Dominic, **The Birth of Christianity**, 1998, Harper San Francisco

Crossan, John Dominic, **The Historical Jesus**, 1991, Harper San Francisco

De Selincourt, Aubrey (tr.), **The Early History of Rome**
— Livy, 1971, Penguin Books

Fiorenza, Elisabeth Schussler, **Bread Not Stone**, 1984,
Beacon Press

Fiorenza, Elisabeth Schussler, **Jesus: Miriam's Child,
Sophia's Prophet**, 1994, Continuum

Fredriksen, Paula, **From Jesus to Christ** (2nd ed.), 2000,
Yale University

Funk, Robert W., **Honest to Jesus**, 1996, Harper San
Francisco

Funk, Robert W.; Hoover, Roy W., et. al, **The Five
Gospels**, 1993, Macmillan

Jeremias, Joachim, **The Sermon on the Mount,** 1961,
Fortress

Mack, Burton L., **The Lost Gospel**, 1993, Harper Collins

Meier, John P., **A Marginal Jew**, 1991, Doubleday

Rubenstein, Richard E., **When Jesus Became God,** 1999, Harcourt Brace

Sanders, E.P., **The Historical Figure of Jesus**, 1993, Penguin Books

Wills, Garry, **A Necessary Evil,** 1999, Simon & Schuster

## ABOUT THE AUTHOR

**Harry T. Cook** is rector of St. Andrew's Episcopal Church in Clawson, Michigan, and a former journalist, editor and columnist. He is known for his teaching ministry in biblical studies and for his provocative and often controversial sermons.

He is a graduate of Albion (Mich.) College and Garrett-Evangelical Theological Seminary at Northwestern University in Evanston, Ill.

Cook is also the author of *Christianity Beyond Creeds,* an analysis of traditional beliefs in contemporary terms, and *Sermons of a Devoted Heretic,* a collection of Sunday homilies that offer hope to people in doubt.